What?

Has the author really written twenty-one other books?

NONFICTION

Hank Greenberg

The Eastern Stars

The Food of a Younger Land

The Last Fish Tale

Nonviolence

The Big Oyster

1968

Salt

The Basque History of the World

Cod

A Chosen Few

A Continent of Islands

ANTHOLOGY

Choice Cuts

FICTION

Edible Stories

Boogaloo on 2nd Avenue

*The White Man in the Tree
and Other Stories*

TRANSLATION

Belly of Paris by Emile Zola

FOR CHILDREN

The Story of Salt

The Girl Who Swam to Euskadi

The Cod's Tale

World Without Fish

What?

Are These Really the Twenty
Most Important Questions
in Human History?

Mark Kurlansky

B L O O M S B U R Y
LONDON · BERLIN · NEW YORK · SYDNEY

First published in Great Britain 2011

Copyright © 2011 by Mark Kurlansky

The moral right of the author has been asserted

Bloomsbury Publishing Plc
36 Soho Square
London W1D 3QY

www.bloomsbury.com

Bloomsbury Publishing, London, Berlin, New York and Sydney

A CIP catalogue record for this book is available from the British Library

ISBN 978 1 4088 1575 5

10 9 8 7 6 5 4 3 2 1

Printed in Great Britain by Clays Ltd, St Ives plc, Bungay, Suffolk

To what's her name? Or was it what's his name?

What does this say?

Sie sind so jung, so vor allem Anfang, und ich möchte Sie, so gut es ich kann, bitten, lieber Herr, Geduld zu habeb gegen alles Ungelöste in Ihrem Herzen und zu versuchen, *die Fragen selbst* liebzuhaben wie verschlossene Stuben und wie Bücher, die in einer sehr fremden Sprache geschrieben sind. Forschen Sie jetzt nicht nach den Antworten, die Ihnen nicht gegeben werden können, weil Sie sie nicht leben könnten. Und es handelt sich darum, alles zu leben. *Leben* Sie jetzt die Fragen. Vielleicht leben Sie dann allmählich, ohne es zu merken, eines fernen Tages in die Antwort hinein.

—Rainer Maria Rilke, *Briefe an einen jungen Dichter*

"What's going on in there?"

What's in this book?

Are these the twenty most important questions in human history,

or is this just the Table of Contents?

Question One: How to Begin?   1

Question Two: How Many?   5

Question Three: How?   9

Question Four: Why?   11

Question Five: What?   19

Question Six: So?   25

Question Seven: Nu?   29

Question Eight: Where?   33

Question Nine: When?   37

Question Ten: Isn't It?   41

Question Eleven: Thralls?   43

Question Twelve: Huh?   47

Question Thirteen: Is This Unlucky?   51

Question Fourteen: Brooklyn?   53

Question Fifteen: Who?   57

Question Sixteen: What Did Freud Want?   61

Question Seventeen: Should I?   65

Question Eighteen: Do I Dare ?   69

Question Nineteen: Where Are You Going?   71

Question Twenty: What Do We Hate
                  About Children?   75

Whom Do I Thank?   81

Is This an Index of Proper Names?   83

What?

"Is a book an answer, or is it a question?"

How to Begin?

Did you ever thumb through a stack of the great books and look to see how many begin with a question? Isn't such a book hard to find? What does it tell us that neither the bible of capitalism, Adam Smith's eighteenth-century *The Wealth of Nations,* nor the bible of communism, Karl Marx's nineteenth-century *Capital*, nor for that matter, the Bible itself, begins with a question? After all, if we don't start with a question, how can we find an answer?

"Suppose no one asked a question," Gertrude Stein postulated; "what would be the answer?" Don't we need questions to get answers? And shouldn't we distrust an answer that comes without a question? An answer without a question—wasn't that Albert Camus's definition

of charm, "a way of getting the answer yes without having asked any clear question"?

Is there an actual shortage of questions in literature
or is it in part that we don't see them? Do we use question marks because without them we do not recognize a
question when we see it? Did Gertrude Stein disagree
when she asked, "A question is a question, anybody can
know that a question is a question and so why add to it
the question mark when it is already there when the
question is already there in the writing"? Isn't this how I
have always felt about exclamation points?!?

Why do we read books, or as Virginia Woolf asked
in *Jacob's Room*: "What do we seek through millions of
pages?"? Couldn't it be argued that all books are
intended as answers, though only a few of them state the
question? Isn't it in the nature of human beings, as
wolves hunt in packs and giant whales migrate with the
seasons, to search for answers? Don't we need to ask
questions in order to get answers? Isn't everybody too
eager to *tell* us without first pondering the uncertainties?

"Why should not we also enjoy an original relationship to the universe?" What is the challenge unleashed
in this opening question of Ralph Waldo Emerson's 1841

essay "Nature"? To achieve such an original relationship, wouldn't we have to ask once again all of the great questions that have been asked before? "Why," Emerson asks, "should not we have a poetry and a philosophy of insight and not of tradition, and a religion of revelation to us and not the history of theirs?" Would not such a new and original way of thinking require a great ability to ask those great questions? Why are we here? Why is all of this here? Why do we die? What is death? What does it mean that outer space is infinite and what is after infinity? What is the significance of winter and spring? What is the significance of bird flight, why does matter decay, and how is our life different from that of a mosquito? Is there an end to these questions or is questioning as infinite as space? Is our questioning skill up to this task or must we depend on better questioners that have gone before us?

Why is Plato the rare thinker who does start with a question? Doesn't it set the mind spinning to be immediately confronted with a question, for example, in the opening line of *Laws*: "Tell me, stranger, is a God or some man supposed to be the author of your laws?"? Wouldn't such a question lead to a far-ranging discussion of government and laws, their purpose, authority, and rightful boundaries?

What is memorable about the writers we call the great thinkers? Isn't asking great questions and the quality of the questions they ask what sets them apart? There are great writers who do not ask great questions, but are they considered great thinkers?

How Many?

What was the first question?

Was it: "Where is the food?"? And if so, doesn't that mean that "where?" was in some sense the first question? Does it all come down to the number one lesson taught to freshmen journalists—that there are six questions: Who? What? When? Where? Why? How? Was it really believed that the answers to these six questions made a complete story? Then are these the only questions, and everything else is a refinement?

Or are there other questions, questions that are more complex, questions for which there is no consensus on answers, or questions whose answers are so troubling that we keep asking them as a way to avoid the answer? When the French aristocrat Alexis-Charles-Henri

"Why can't I find anything but the Big Dipper?"

Clérel de Tocqueville—by the way, didn't he have too many names and were his parents people who couldn't make up their minds?—analyzed the strengths and weaknesses of American democracy in the 1830s, wasn't the big question about America: "Can it be believed that democracy, after having destroyed feudalism and overthrown kings, will retreat in the face of the bourgeois and the wealthy?"? Almost two centuries of American democracy later, doesn't this question still lay here like the package no one wants to open? How many of Tocqueville's troubling questions have been answered? How many really good questions ever do get answered? Or is it more important that they get asked?

"How am I different than a bee?"

How?

In a world that seems devoid of absolute certainties, how can we make declarative statements? Don't we all risk one day asking, as Colonel Brandon does in the Jane Austen novel *Sense and Sensibility*, "Where so many hours have been spent in convincing myself that I am right, is there not some reason to fear I may be wrong?"?

How do we know anything for certain? Aren't even our beliefs, our opinions, subject to change and, as Marcel Proust put it, aren't they "as eternally fluid as the sea itself"? Is it true, as Proust wrote, that "all our resolutions are made in a state of mind that is not going to last"? Or am I completely wrong about this? Now isn't that a question we often forget to ask?

Aren't we only on solid ground when asking questions? And yet, don't all of us make more statements than questions? Is this why we have not been able to find certainties?

Could this be what the seventeenth-century French philosopher René Descartes was getting at in his *Discourse on Method* when he questioned his existence? If we can't know anything for certain, how do we even know that we exist? Wasn't his conclusion—cogito, ergo sum, I think, therefore I am—an attempt to answer this question? And wasn't this answer an assertion that the act of asking is proof enough of your existence? Then, doesn't it follow that people who don't ask questions have no proof of their existence? Of course couldn't you exist anyway, even if you couldn't prove it? But aren't we better off asking the question just to have the proof? On the other hand, isn't it likely that the kind of people who don't ask questions are not likely to worry about whether or not they exist?

Question Four

Why?

Didn't another philosopher, the nineteenth-century German Friedrich Nietzsche, present a very different concept of the fundamental question when he asked, "Why I am so wise?"? Or is this the same question that Descartes asked, only asked in a German way instead of French? Or was Nietzsche's question merely the nineteenth-century version of Descartes' seventeenth-century one? And how French was Descartes? Why was all his important work done after he settled in Holland? Was it Holland that made him that way? Then again, why did German-born Nietzsche insist that he was really Polish?

Did Nietzsche ever answer his question? If not, would that be the reason he was so wise? Didn't he ask a

"Why do I think I am not alone?"

lot more questions than he answered? Didn't he begin his autobiography, *Ecce Homo*, by asking who he is? Is it really an autobiography, though, since he never really answers this question either?

Might he have posed another question: Why am I so difficult? Couldn't that question be read several ways and might not all of them be true? Does the fact that his last name has a ratio of two consonants for each vowel, and, in fact, five uninterrupted consonants in a row make Nietzsche difficult? Or does it just make him difficult to spell?

Is it because he was a philosopher that Nietzsche asked so many questions and gave so few answers? Aren't philosophy and religion both ways of asking questions? Or are they opposing ways? Why did Nietzsche, the philosopher, so dislike religion? Did he dislike its questions or simply feel disdain for its answers? Is that why he wrote, "God is a crude answer"? And why he went on to say that God is "a piece of indelicacy against us thinkers—fundamentally even a crude prohibition to us: You shall not think!"?

Could a man with limited answers have limitless questions? Why, for example, did Nietzsche ask, "Has a woman who knew she was well dressed ever caught a cold?"? And why did a man who asked so many questions insist that he did not want answers? Why did he say, "There is a great deal I do not want to know"?

Is it significant that most historians have concluded that Hitler was lying when he claimed to have read Nietzsche, whereas Richard Nixon is thought to have told the truth—about having read Nietzsche?

Why did Nietzsche keep repeating the question: "Have I been understood?"? Did he see that a thinker who rejected God, religion, and morality—practicing what he termed "philosophy with a hammer"—could be easily misused? When he wrote, "One day there will be associated with my name the recollection of something frightful—of a crisis like no other before on earth, of the profoundest collision of conscience," did he foresee that Hitler and the Nazi holocaust would invoke his writing? Is this fair? Should Karl Marx be blamed for Joseph Stalin? Should Adam Smith be blamed for robber barons? Can George Washington be held accountable for George W. Bush? If after reading this book, someone drove everyone around to the brink of madness by ever after limiting all intercourse to questions, never offering answers, would that be my fault? Can an idea be blamed for those who misuse it? Can a question be blamed for the wrong answer?

If it is important to ask questions, is it equally important to answer them? Doesn't questioning have its own value? But are there questions that shouldn't be asked? And if they are asked, should they always be answered? Wouldn't marriage be the kind of relationship where questions sometimes should not be asked, or at least not answered? In the 1942 film *Casablanca*, when Paul Henreid asks his wife, Ingrid Bergman, "Dear, were you lonely when I was in the concentration camp?"— isn't this an excellent example of the kind of question that should not be asked?

How did Arthur Schopenhauer, the nineteenth-century German philosopher, explain that nature never appears to answer our questions? "Can her failure to reply ever be for any reason other than we have asked the wrong question?" Is that why some questions remain unanswered?

Is a question always a search for an answer? Don't writers sometimes ask the most obvious questions to send the reader looking for the answer that the writer already has? Isn't that what Jean-Jacques Rousseau—a great questioner—was doing when he asked, "There is peace in dungeons, but is that enough to make dungeons desirable?"? And isn't that what a West Indian slave named Mary Prince was doing in 1831 when she had her thoughts on slavery written down and published so that the people of England might finally hear from a slave on slavery? She didn't have any doubts about her assessment of slavery, so why then did she ask the following questions?

> How can slaves be happy when they have the halter round their neck and the whip on their back? and are disgraced and thought no more of than beasts?—and are separated from their mothers, and husbands, and children, and sisters just as cattle are sold? and is it happiness for a driver in the field to take down his wife or sister or child, and strip them and whip them in such a disgraceful manner?

What would happen when the reader tried to answer such questions? Didn't Mary Prince, who didn't know how to write a single word, understand very well how to use questions, understand the power of the word "why"? Why was "why" a word frequently used against the idea of slavery? Could the word "why" be ironic, as when the nineteenth-century Haitian poet Massillon Coicou, in a poem called "The Slave's Lament," asks, "Why am I a Negro? Oh, why am I black?"? But can't "why" also be, as Mary Prince showed, defiantly rhetorical, as in the poem "Ghetto" by the twentieth-century Guadeloupian poet Guy Tirolien:

Why should I confine myself
to the image
they would fix me in?

"*Do I make any more sense than this painting?*"

What?

Could it be that it is less important to know which question goes first than to know which one goes last—the ultimate question? If *who*ers are gossips, *when*ers impatient, *why*ers dreamers, *where*-ers lost, and *how*ers pragmatists, is it the *what*ers who cut to the heart of things? What am I talking about? What is this book? What is a book? Isn't "what is writing?" a more fundamental question than George Orwell's when he asked why he wrote? Doesn't *what* usually trump *why*?

What is at the heart of intellectual pursuit? Is it "what?"? If so, shouldn't the first sentence of this paragraph be read as a statement? Some might say that "why?" is the root question of science, but isn't the scientific why just the hypothesis that leads to answering the real goal of science, which is "what?"? Isn't this similar to the way history appears to be about "when?" while it is ultimately, again, about "what?"? If the questions at "the irreducible core to a story about the past" according to historian Margaret MacMillan are "What happened and in what order?"—then doesn't this mean we really want to know "what?"?

When Marcus Garvey wanted to completely change the history and image of black people, didn't he choose to title his essay: "Who and What is a Negro?"? Does this mean that "who?" in the hands of a revolutionary also leads, then, to "what?"?

Wouldn't you think a poet would be a *why*er? Then why was the great Spanish poet Federico García Lorca such a chronic *what*er? Why does that Spanish word *qué* keep turning up at the beginning of his sentences? Does he not ask the fundamental poet's question when he wrote, "What is the use, I wonder, of ink, paper and poetry?"? When a dying ant sadly declares, "I have seen the stars," what do the other ants reply? "Qué son las estrellas?" What are stars? Why, for that matter, do snails, such a rudimentary, basic animal, keep appearing in his poems? Why did he write: "They have brought me a snail. / Inside it sings / a map-green ocean"? And why describe autumn: "With small white snails"? Was García Lorca a *what*er because he questioned basic, fundamental things? Isn't that a *what*er for you? Did that make him a dangerous man? Is that why Franco, fighting to establish a fascist dictatorship, had him murdered? If it seems clear that police states don't like questioners, are they especially distrustful of *what*ers?

Didn't Langston Hughes in a 1951 poem predict decades of urban uprisings by asking what? "What happens to a dream deferred?"

Wasn't José Martí, who was the father of Cuban independence and a true rebel, also a great *what*er? Didn't he ask, in an article praising another rebel, Ralph Waldo Emerson, "For what man who is master of himself does not laugh at a king?"? Is this not a dangerous man? What did he ask his general, Máximo Gómez, whom he feared had dreams of a military dictatorship? "What are we, General?" What? "Are we the heroic modest servants of an idea that fires our hearts, the loyal friends of a nation in distress? Or are we bold and fortune-favored *caudillos* who with whip in hand and spurs on our heels prepare to bring war to a nation in order to take possession of it ourselves?" What?

Why is the question "what?" so fundamental? What is it about "what?"? What happens when Jean-Anthelme Brillat-Savarin, in his great early nineteenth-century book on food, *The Physiology of Taste*, asks a question: "Are truffles digestible?"? Isn't that a good question to ask before eating a truffle? But is it as fundamental as his earlier question: "What is meant by food?"?

Isn't an even more fundamental food question: "What is it?"? Why do you hear this all the time in Israeli food stores? "Mah ha zeh?" "What is it?" And why is the answer always another question: "Mah?"?

"What is it?"

"What?"

Are Israelis intrinsically *what*ers? Are they people who question fundamentals? Is the most ubiquitous question the most important question, and if so, doesn't this mean that Israelis believe that the most important question is "what?"? Could this be why they walk around all day repeatedly saying, "Mah? Mah?"? "What? What?"

Does such questioning get us anywhere? Or is "what?" not a question at all but a statement? Or do they just think "what?" is the first question? Then why do they not move on? Is it because "what?" has not been adequately answered?

Isn't the important question: "Why?"? But doesn't that just leave us open to the Talmudic answer: "Why not?"? Is that just the negative version of the same question? Or is it the positive version? Do Israelis prefer to ask "what?" because they know even the Talmud can't reverse that one on them the way it can "why?"?

"How do I explain all this?"

Question Six

So?

Haven't Jews always been great questioners? Isn't the Talmud, especially the part written around the year 500 called the Gemara, an example of this? Why does it constantly pose questions? Is it because the Talmud is an attempt to compile all the rabbinic teachings, and the rabbinical style of teaching is posing questions? Or do rabbis teach like this because this is how the Talmud is written?

When I asked a rabbi why the Talmud instructs fathers to teach their sons how to swim, why did he answer with a question: "The Talmudic answer would be: 'Why not?'"?

Why does the Talmud frame answers in terms of questions? For example, why does the Talmud say, "Who is wise? One who learns from all"? Wouldn't it have been easier to say, "One who learns from everyone is wise"? How many of these Q&As are in the Talmud, including: "Who is rich? He that rejoices in his portion," "Who is a hero? He who conquers his urge"?

Is it a coincidence that the Haggadah—the guide to the Passover seder that explains the holiday to children by having them ask four questions—was first conceived during the same period as the Talmud? And why do we always refer to the "four questions" when actually they ask five?

Doesn't the Talmud ask so many questions because one of its original inspirations was Hillel, the great first-century rabbi, who was a great questioner in his own right? And aren't there good reasons that some of his questions are still remembered today? "If I am not for myself, who will be for me? If I am not for others, what am I? And if not now, when?" Were these his best questions? Or are they just his most famous?

Why does the Talmud use a different word for question than *she'eilah*, the ancient Hebrew word for question that is used in the Torah that has its roots in asking for a gift? Why does the Talmud use the word *kushiya*, which comes from the Hebrew word *kusheh*, meaning hard? Is this hard as in hard as a rock—something in nature that is durable and impenetrable, that can only be chipped away at? Is the Talmud expressing the notion that an answer is something you must earn? Is the Talmud saying what young newspaper reporters used to be taught, that all questions should be hard? But would newspapers want to follow that to Talmudic lengths and say that no good question can be completely answerable?

Is it because of centuries of Talmudic thinking that in the Yiddish language the speaker's voice raises in pitch toward the end of a sentence, making even statements sound like questions? Could this also be why Yiddish has so many one-word questions: *nu?* meaning "well?" or *azoy?* meaning "so?"?

"Should I look more closely?"

Nu?

What does it mean that so many of the really great questioners came from ancient civilizations? Are we losing the ability to ask good questions? Or have we lost the understanding that knowledge begins with a question? Is it surprising that the Chinese, who claim to have invented almost everything first, asked good questions? Did they invent the question? Who can say? Why don't they claim it anyway?

Does the craft of questioning predate *The Analects of Confucius*, which were written over a more than thirty-year period in the sixth and fifth centuries BC? Wouldn't it be significant that even Confucius predates the *Analects*, since they were written down later by his followers? Isn't it possible that Confucius was an even better questioner than they remembered? And was it Confucius or was it his followers who originated the style of Chinese thought that was centered on formulating great questions? Was this style used in the debates of wise men sponsored by the government because these debates always had followers of Confucius on one side? When the teenage Han emperor Zhaodi, who sponsored one such debate of sixty wise men in 81 BC, asked the Confucians how the state should raise profits, why did the Confucians answer, "Why must your majesty use the word 'profit?'"? When asked how the state should finance its military, why did they answer, "Why do we need military spending?"? Was it the use of questions that made this debate, ostensibly about the wisdom of state monopolies on salt and iron, become such a far-reaching discussion of good government that it is still studied today? Is it the way questions were answered with more questions that has kept this debate alive? After all, wouldn't answering with answers tend to end a debate?

How influential has this been in Chinese thinking, this mental habit of couching ideas in questions? A millennium later, didn't Kuo Hsi begin his famous essay on painting landscapes, "Shan shui Hsün," with the question: "Why does a virtuous man take delight in landscapes?"? Isn't the rest of the essay an answer to this?

Couldn't even what Jesus called the golden rule be traced back to an ancient Chinese question? When was this golden rule best stated? Was it when Jesus presented it as a rule stating, according to the Book of Matthew, "Do unto others as you would have them do unto you"? Or when Rabbi Hillel, the famous scholar of the day, who was Jesus's source, presented it as a riddle about explaining the entire Torah while standing on one foot? Or was it best presented in the fourth century BC by the Chinese anti-Confucianist philosopher Mozi, who posed it as a question, asking, "For if every man were to regard the persons of others as his own, who would inflict pain and injury on others?"? And doesn't this progression from question to riddle to rule show a historic shift away from questions to more rigid assertions? Doesn't this move us away from a rational choice based on free will to an obedient response to a moral command? Which is the stronger society, the one where people act well because it makes sense, or the one where people act well because they are supposed to?

Do newer religions ask questions? Where are the questions in Protestantism, one of the newest and least ritualistic of religions? Doesn't the cantata, the choral piece before a Protestant sermon, start the sermon, Jewish-style, with a question? And aren't Bach's stunningly beautiful cantatas, with lyrics from the German Lutheran writer Erdmann Neumeister, full of very large questions? Doesn't one of the largest questions appear in the opening line of Bach's Cantata no. 8—"Liebster Gott, wann werd ich sterben?" Dearest God, when shall I die?

Where?

Where is Persia, and why isn't it called that anymore? What better illustrates the lack of Western understanding of Iran than the fact that few Westerners are familiar with the single most important book in Iranian literature, *Shahnameh: The Persian Book of Kings*? Why does this book, a massive epic about the pre-Islamic kings of Persia written by the tenth-century poet Abolqasem Ferdowsi that took most of his life to write, start with a question: "What does the Persian poet say about the first man to seek the crown of world sovereignty?"? Does it start with a question because his answer is that there is little known about the first king? What better way to launch a nine-hundred-page epic? Would a statement be able to launch a work of such sweep? What

"Where am I going?"

statement would be up to the task? Isn't a question the only honest way to begin a story that starts in an unknown mythical time? If we are going to admit that we don't know much about it, wouldn't it be false to start with a statement?

How many Americans even know where Iran is? Isn't the often-noted failure of Americans to understand world events because of a poor knowledge of geography, simply a failure to ask the question: "Where?"?

But, on the other hand, don't people spend too much time asking "where?"? Where was it made? Where were you born? Where is the border to be drawn? Isn't much of racism and extreme nationalism a result of spending too much time asking "where?"?

Still, isn't the answer to the question "where?" often an important thing to know? Isn't it troubling that many of the young people sent to fight distant wars do not know exactly where these countries are? And if a devastating hurricane is about to make landfall, wouldn't it be a good idea to know where? If we receive a telephone call and don't know where the person is calling from, isn't "where?" at least the second question? Don't we ask "who?" and then "where?"? Who is it? Where are you calling from? Can we fully understand the conversation without first knowing from where the call is coming? Isn't "where" the context that makes things understandable?

Is it surprising that Thomas Merton, a Trappist monk who studied Asian religion and was a great questioner, would often ask "where?"? Isn't it natural that a seeker such as Merton would ask this question, as in when he is contemplating the riddle of heaven and earth, which can do everything and yet do nothing?

> *Where is the man who can attain*
> *To this non doing?*

And didn't Merton have other "where" questions such as "Where is Tao?" and "Where's your virtue gone?"? If you could answer that question wouldn't you know a great deal about yourself? But was his ultimate question from his seventy books not a *where* question at all, but, "Am I a man to imitate?"?

When?

Isn't it true that while warfare most often begins with a declaration, dialogue, including the dialogue that inevitably follows war, is best begun with a question? So wouldn't it be better to start with a question? Could the use of a question instead of a declaration lead to skipping the war part?

For example, wouldn't it have been more productive, perhaps even have averted eight years of bloodshed, if in 1776 Thomas Jefferson, rather than writing a Declaration of Independence, had written a Questioning of Colonial Ties? Did Jefferson start off with "when," even though he didn't use it as a question, because "When?" is the favorite question of impatient revolutionaries? Is it redundant to call revolutionaries impa-

"When?"

tient? Is it the lack of patience that makes them revolutionary? Instead of beginning "When, in the course of human events, it becomes necessary for one people to dissolve the political bonds which have connected them with another," what if he had begun: "When, in the course of human events, does it become necessary for one people to dissolve the political bonds which have connected them with another?"?

But did he want to play that old game of trying to get an Englishman to answer a question? Was the Declaration founded in the knowledge that the English don't use declarative sentences—that the best answer he could have hoped for would have been: "Now might be the right time, mightn't it?"?

"How does this end?"

Isn't It?

If there is a people who have perfected the craft of the gratuitous interrogative, wouldn't that be the British? Or is it just the English? How do they manage to turn everything into a question? They do, don't they? Could it be that the failure of the Empire has taught them there are no certainties in the world? And if that is true, wouldn't it be better to ask than to state? But why do I always suspect that the English, just like the French, are not looking for answers and that they are only asking because they think it is good manners? Do they find declarative sentences rude? Is not a casual conversation on a London street entirely made up of questions?

"How are you?"

"And you?"

"A bit of an awful day, isn't it?"

"Well, it's rained for a week, hasn't it?"

"Just bloody awful, isn't it?"

"Yes it is, isn't it?"

"Oh well, is it getting late?"

"Is it?"

"We can't really spend the day chatting, can we?"

"It would be lovely if we could, though, wouldn't it?"

Is it my imagination or is there a contentious undercurrent of one-upmanship here? Are both of the interlocutors trying to somehow trick the other into a declarative sentence? Why? Is it to see who has the best manners?

Thralls?

What did it accomplish? Was it worth it? How did it happen? How could we have stopped it? Did so many have to die?

Aren't there many questions to be asked after a war? Isn't the big one: "What do we do now?"? Or "How do we make this worth it?"? Or the one the average soldier always asks, as one did in Norman Mailer's 1948 World War II novel *The Naked and the Dead*, "Shall the GIs have died in vain?"? How is it possible that this question can be asked after every war and yet never be answered? Is it because if it were answered it would mean the end of war? Or do soldiers keep answering it, but no one wants to hear their answer? Is that why no one wants to hear

"Will tomorrow be different?"

from rank and file soldiers—why they are available for parades but not for interviews?

Wouldn't you expect a lot of questions to have been asked after World War II? When a book called *Treasury for the Free World* was put together in 1946 with contributions from leaders and writers around the world—nothing from regular soldiers, of course—with an introduction by Ernest Hemingway, wouldn't you have thought that this would be a book full of questions?

So what did Charles de Gaulle ask about the new world to be built? "How can one imagine it without France?" But when the aptly named de Gaulle talked about France, wasn't he usually talking about himself?

When, in the same book, the poet Carl Sandburg recalled the words of Lincoln, "We must disenthrall ourselves," didn't he say it's a noble sentiment but what does it mean?

And what is a thrall? And who are thralls?

But at that moment at the end of World War II, would it be surprising that the best questions came from a German, Thomas Mann? Wasn't he always a great questioner? Didn't he ask in the foreword to his seven-hundred-page novel, *The Magic Mountain*, set in a tuberculosis rest clinic where absolutely nothing happens: "When was a story short on diversion or long on boredom simply because of the time and space required in the telling?"? And didn't he begin his equally long novel, *Buddenbrooks*, with the question: "What does this mean?"? And isn't that the essential question?

Could it be that Mann asked the most fundamental question of 1946: "How will it be to belong to a nation, to work in a spiritual tradition of a nation...under whose desperate, megalomaniac effort to become a nation the world has had to suffer so much!"? Why, though, did he end that question with an exclamation mark? Now, more than sixty years later—after Vietnam, Bosnia, Rwanda, Iraq, and Afghanistan—is that question as relevant as Sandburg's question for 1946?

Have I, have you, been too silent?
Is there an easy crime of silence?

Huh?

Why did Ernest Hemingway like to start a story with a question? Did this make him a good questioner? What was the purpose of these questions? Was it to lead to other questions? Then does the reader, like the writer, start with a question? What questions are provoked by Hemingway's questions?

Why does he begin "The Short Happy Life of Francis Macomber" with "Will you have lime juice or lemon squash?"?

Or "Fifty Grand" with "How are you going yourself, Jack?"?

Or "Today is Friday" with "You tried the red?"?

Or "The Sea Change" with "'Alright,' said the man, 'What about it?'"?

"What has happened to my brain?

Is Hemingway leading the reader at the start of these stories to the question: "What about it?"? Or "How are you going yourself?"? Doesn't the reader then ask, "What the hell are you trying to say, Hem?"? In other words, "Huh?"

What kind of a question is "Huh?"? Why does such a word exist? Isn't its existence an affirmation of the importance of asking questions? Doesn't it say that even if you do not know what to ask, just asking is of value in itself?

"Why me?"

Question Thirteen

Is This Unlucky?

Why is thirteen unlucky? Suppose you don't believe it is unlucky or you don't even believe in luck? Isn't "believe" the important word here? Doesn't belief always mean that you don't know for certain? How can we know things for certain? If we could, would we need to have questions? And if we could, would we need luck? What is luck? Is it worth playing with this? Given the risks and uncertainties, wouldn't it be best to move on to question fourteen?

"Is somebody there?"

ℬrooklyn?

Isn't it interesting that the great definer of American-
ness, the man who heard it singing, Walt Whitman, was
a guy from Brooklyn, a place many would say has little in
common with America?

Did defining America, hearing it sing, have something to do with his tendency to ask questions? Did he
start by asking, "What is America?"? Isn't this question
often asked by people from Brooklyn?

Wasn't there something fundamental about Whitman's questions? Is that why I as a writer remember his
poem "What Am I, After All?"

> *What am I after all but a child, pleas'd with the sound of*
> *my own name?*

But for a writer, didn't Whitman ask even more fun-damental questions, such as these?

What think you I take my pen in hand to record?
The battleship, perfect-model'd, majestic, that I saw pass
*   the offing to-day under full sail?*
The splendor of the past day? Or the splendor of the night
*   that envelops me?*
Or the vaunted glory and growth of the great city spread
*   around me?*

And how does Whitman answer this in one word? What is the next line? Isn't it "—no"?

Aren't we driven by a fear of being nobody? A fear of the answer to the question: "Who am I?"? Isn't this why, when facing arrogance, the question of choice is "Who the hell do you think you are?"? Who can answer that one for sure? But aren't there worse questions? Even if you found that you were nobody, would that be so terrible? Wouldn't it still be better than not existing at all? Is it so bad to be a nobody among nobodies? Is that what the poet Emily Dickinson thought when she wrote her poem "I'm Nobody! Who are you?"?

> *Are you—Nobody—Too?*
> *Then there's a pair of us?*

"Who is it?"

Who?

Can I confess something? Is it significant that as a student I got Dante Gabriel Rosetti's name wrong, that I thought it was Gabriela Rossetti and that he was a woman? What is certain about Dante Gabriel Rossetti? Was he a British poet even though his Italian parents named him after an Italian poet? Was he even a poet, since he was best known for his paintings? Can we at least say that if it is true that a poet should ask questions, he was one?

> *What of her glass without her? The blank gray*
> *There where the pool hid blind of the moon's face,*
> *Her dress without her? The tossed empty space*

Of cloud-rack whence the moon has passed away
Her paths without her?

Don't poets ask questions? Didn't John Keats ask why?

Why did I laugh tonight?

Didn't he ask where?

Where are the songs of Spring? Ay, where are they?

and

WHERE be ye going, you Devon maid?
And what have ye there i' the basket?
Ye tight little fairy, just fresh from the dairy,
Will ye give me some cream if I ask it?

And above all, who?

Lo! who dares say, "Do this"? Who dares call down

My will from its high purpose? Who say, "Stand,"
Or, "Go"?

But doesn't just the act of quoting Keats raise the question of who? Who can quote Keats and be sure it isn't Shelley? Is it important to be sure because of the certainty that someone will say, "No, that's Shelley"? Although wouldn't it be wiser for that person to say, "Isn't that Shelley?"?

How do we distinguish between two English romantic poets who lived about the same time, and who both died very young? Was Shelley a questioner like Keats? Didn't he ask how?

How shall ever one like me
Win thee back again?

And art?

Art thou pale for weariness
Of climbing heaven and gazing on the earth,
Wandering companionless

Among the stars that have a different birth,
And ever changing, like a joyless eye
That finds no object worth its constancy?

But was he really a questioner the way Keats was? Does even Shelley's poem "The Question"—that's Shelley, right, not Keats?—ask much, aside from who to give the nosegay to at the end? Couldn't we say that Keats was the one who really asked questions?

Or was the more essential "who" question asked by Spain's famous Generation of '98 poet Antonio Machado, when he said, "Answer my question—Who do I speak to?"? Or did he get even deeper into the matter of "who" later in the poem when he asked, "What does it matter who I am?"? And isn't this a fitting question for a man whose name was even longer than Tocqueville's—Antonio Cipriano José María y Francisco de Santa Ana Machado y Ruiz?

Question Sixteen

What Did Freud Want?

Is this what becomes of a man who was adored by his mother, his wife, and his three daughters? What was Sigmund Freud's great unresolvable question—his *"grosse Frage"*? Wasn't it really, as he said, "Was will das Weib?"— What do women want? Isn't that one of those perennial questions that keeps coming up from time to time, for example when Marilyn Monroe married Joe DiMaggio? But doesn't it make you feel sad about Freud? Is the question just that what women want is a psychoanalyst who understands them? Or is this too much of a generalization? Isn't it unlikely that women all want the same thing, even if to men, at least this one, they seem to talk as though they do when they get together with each

61

"What does she want?"

other? Did Freud read Nietzsche, who asked why women are considered deep? Was his answer—"Because one can never discover any bottom to them"—the answer Freud was seeking?

"So what was the question?"

Should I?

Wasn't William Shakespeare, more than most writers, famous for his questions? Shouldn't a lot of his titles have question marks after them? *Much Ado About Nothing?* Or *All's Well That Ends Well?* Or even *Richard III?* Isn't there a question of legitimacy there?

If Shakespeare did not have a profound appreciation for questions, would he have had Julius Caesar go out on a question? "Et tu, Brute?" Another question: Even if they are Romans, they have been talking all throughout the play in English, so how come Caesar's dying question is in Latin? Is it because he is really serious about it? When your best friend is found in a plot to murder you, that would be a moment to ask questions in Latin wouldn't it?

Why is anti-Semitism the subject for which Shakespeare unleashes one of his longest outpourings of the interrogative?

> Hath not a Jew eyes? hath not a Jew hands, organs, dimensions, senses, affections, passions? fed with the same food, hurt with the same weapons, subject to the same diseases, healed by the same means, warmed and cooled by the same winter and summer, as a Christian is? If you prick us, do we not bleed? if you tickle us, do we not laugh? if you poison us, do we not die? and if you wrong us, shall we not revenge?

Why is it that none of these questions really require an answer? Is it the same reason that the French always refer to anti-Semitism as "The Jewish Question"? Or was Shakespeare simply trying to write a credible Jewish character and agreeing with me that Jews speak in questions a lot?

What was Shakespeare's most important question? Wasn't it given to Prince Hamlet? "To be or not to be"? Is that really *the* question? Isn't it just a more self-centered or depressed or hamstrung version of Descartes' "cogito, ergo sum"? Wasn't Hamlet's problem that he was lost in questions? Did he spend too much time asking them? Can you spend too much time asking questions?

"Do I dare to eat a friend?"

Do I Dare?

Doesn't this inevitably lead to T. S. Eliot's J. Alfred Prufrock? If T. S. Eliot had not intended for his readers to ask questions, wouldn't he have been more forthcoming about his full name? And why else would he start his Prufrock poem in Italian, even though he knows we can't read it? And isn't Prufrock, whose first name, like that of the author, is only alluded to, even more lost in the interrogative than Hamlet? "Do I dare? Do I dare?" Why does he keep asking that? Between what to eat and how to wear his hair, is there anything this guy can decide on? But if he is lost in questions like Prince Hamlet, then why does he say, "I am not Prince Hamlet"? With all this questioning, doesn't it seem that he is? Or is he saying that his questions don't rise to the level of

Hamlet's? Are questions not all equal? Then who is worse, someone who doesn't ask questions, or someone whose questions aren't any good? Or does contemplating this conundrum make me worse than either? Or is this question of who is worse *the* question?

Where Are You Going?

Quo Vadis? Where are you going? Why is this the big question of Catholicism? Why does Peter say "Quo Vadis?" to Jesus? Why would a Hebrew speak Latin to a fellow Hebrew? And what are we to make of the answer: "I'm going to Rome to be crucified"? Is this not a good example of an answer that really only raises more questions? Doesn't it sound very Jewish if what you hear is "Oh, don't worry about me; I'll just go to Rome and get crucified"? But why does he say Rome when he is probably going to Jerusalem, and why would he go there to be crucified? Isn't the question the point?

Isn't it significant that the life of Jesus ended with a question? "My God, why hast thou forsaken me?" Does the fact that this question was recorded in Aramaic and

"Where are we?"

not Latin give it more authenticity? Or is it just that it is a better question than the one he was asked in Latin? Are the best questions unanswerable? Is that the real test of a question? Or is not getting an answer, as Schopenhauer believed, a sign that you are asking the wrong question? Why did God forsake him? Is that the right question? Isn't it the wrong question for a religious person but the central question of agnostics? Wasn't Job tempted to ask this question? Isn't the split between religious people and atheists divided on the answer to this question? If there is a God, why was there a holocaust, a massacre in Rwanda, and why do children die? Isn't this a central question of religion?

But can I ask a different question? Suppose the story had ended there, with Jesus asking this question? Would this have been a good story? Would Christianity ever have developed? Didn't Christian leaders early on sense the problem when they started explaining that he wasn't really asking a question when he said, "Why hast thou forsaken me?"—that he was really saying, "This is my destiny"? Isn't the point that he needs to end on a statement, not a question? Can a good story end on a question? Of course, wasn't this problem solved by not ending there, but instead by having him resurrected into everlasting life? Without that, if it had just ended on that question—"Why hast thou forsaken me?"—where would the story be?

What Do We Hate About Children?

"Is a child to be considered as an individuality, or as an object to be moulded according to the whims and fancies of those about it?" When the nineteenth-century radical Emma Goldman asked this question, wasn't she really asking how much patience we have for questions? For if children are free to express individuality, aren't they likely to express it with endless questions? Have you ever been around the kind of child who, no matter what you say, always responds with "Why?"? Why? Why? Why? Isn't this extremely irritating? Why? (Excuse me?) Isn't it because when faced with such a child, your work is never done, you have to keep coming up with answers? Wouldn't the same be true of any kind of relentless interlocutor: rabbi, poet, philosopher? Isn't this book,

"But why?"

like the life of Jesus, at risk of being unsatisfying if it ends with a question? Are questions what we really want? Aren't questions just the vehicle, and answers ultimately the destinations? And so sooner or later, in this case later, isn't a clear declarative sentence needed?

Yes.

You are so young, and have not even started, and I want to beg you, as strongly as I can, dear sir, to be patient with all that is unsolved in your heart and try to love *the questions themselves* like locked rooms and like books that are written in a very foreign tongue. Do not now seek the answers, which cannot be given to you because you would not be able to live them. And the point is, to live everything. *Live* the questions now. Perhaps you will then gradually, without noticing it, live along some distant day into the answer.

—Rainer Maria Rilke, *Letters to a Young Poet*

"Is there anything else in there?"

Whom Do I Thank?

How can I thank Nancy Miller again? Doesn't it seem as if I have thanked her 347 times already? But what can I do if she keeps doing great work? Should I thank my friend and agent, Charlotte Sheedy? Is it a problem that she doesn't get it? Or should I thank her for championing it even when she doesn't get it? And what about George Gibson, the publisher? Do I thank him? Is that just because I'm so happy to be doing a book with him again? Or is it because he is a great publisher? Or is it just because I like him so much?

Shouldn't I thank Rabbi Rolando Matalon, a great questioner with the rare blend of intellect and kindness? Since he is always full of interesting ideas, should I also thank him for putting me on to the brilliant work of

Avivah Gottlieb Zornberg and especially her dazzling study of the Book of Exodus—*The Particulars of Rapture*? But if I'm going to thank her, shouldn't I then thank Margaret MacMillan who wrote *Dangerous Games*, a book I don't entirely agree with but thoroughly enjoyed for its reasoning and the quality of the questions she asked?

And having thanked these people, what about all the rest? Do I thank Nietsche? Or would spelling his name correctly be enough?

And what about my wife, Marian, and daughter, Talia? Shouldn't I just thank them for answering my question: Why am I here?

Index of Proper Names?

Austen, Jane, 9

Bach, Johann Sebastian, 32
Bergman, Ingrid, 15
Brandon, Colonel, 9
Brillat-Savarin, Jean-
    Anthelme, 22
Bush, George W., 14

Caesar, Julius, 65
Camus, Albert, 1–2
Coicou, Massillon, 17
Confucius, 29, 30

de Gaulle, Charles, 45
Descartes, René, 10, 11, 67
Dickinson, Emily, 54–55
DiMaggio, Joe, 61

Eliot, T. S., 69
Emerson, Ralph Waldo,
    2–3, 21

Ferdowski, Abolqasem, 33
Franco, Francisco, 21
Freud, Sigmund, 61, 62

García Lorca, Federico,
    20, 21
Garvey, Marcus, 20
God, 13, 14, 73
Goldman, Emma, 75
Gómez, Máximo, 21

Hamlet, 66–67, 69–70
Hemingway, Ernest, 45,
    47, 49
Henreid, Paul, 15
Hillel the Elder, Rabbi,
    26, 31
Hitler, Adolf, 14
Hughes, Langston, 21

Jefferson, Thomas, 37
Jesus, 31, 71, 77
Job, 73

Keats, John, 58, 59, 60
Kuo Hsi, 30–31

Lincoln, Abraham, 45

MacMillan, Margaret, 20
Mailer, Norman, 43
Mann, Thomas, 45, 46
Martí, José, 21
Marx, Karl, 1, 14
Merton, Thomas, 36
Monroe, Marilyn, 61
Mozi, 31

Neumeister, Erdmann, 32
Nietzsche, Friedrich, 11,
    13–14, 62
Nixon, Richard, 14

Orwell, George, 19

Peter (apostle), 71
Plato, 3
Prince, Mary, 16, 17
Proust, Marcel, 9

Rosetti, Dante Gabriel, 57
Rousseau, Jean-Jacques, 16

Sandburg, Carl, 45, 46
Santa Ana Machado y
    Ruiz, Antonio Cipri-
    ano José Mariá y
    Francisco de, 60
Schopenhauer, Arthur, 15,
    73
Shakespeare, William, 65,
    66
Shelley, Percy, 59, 60
Smith, Adam, 1, 14
Stalin, Joseph, 14
Stein, Gertrude, 1, 2

Tirolien, Guy, 17
Tocqueville, Alexis de, 5–7,
    60

Washington, George, 14
Whitman, Walt, 53–54

Who is the author of this book?

Is it Mark Kurlansky, the *New York Times* bestselling author of *Cod*, *Salt*, *The Basque History of the World*, *1968*, *The Big Oyster*, and *The Eastern Stars*, among many other books? Will you find out if you visit his Web site at www.markkurlansky.com?